Also by Tony Gentry

The Coal Tower, a novel

Last Rites, stories

YEARNFUL RAVES

50 Poems

by

Tony Gentry

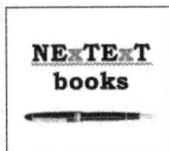

NExTExT
books

Richmond, VA

2020

FOR

Nick & Stephen

ACKNOWLEDGMENTS

Grateful acknowledgment is made to the following publications in which these poems first appeared:

"The Poet's Way" and "For Borges," *The Quarterly*
"Birds in Snow," *Deep South*
"Immigrant Reflection," *Richmond Magazine*
"Truisms," *Sow's Ear Poetry Review*
"River Shadows" and "Your Peach and Mine," *Virginia Bards Poetry Review*
"The Depressive Enumerates," *Minetta Review*
"Liberty Under Repair," *Downtown*
"Subversive Scribble: 2069," "Blackberry Missive" and "If it Serves," *Mad Swirl*
"Figments" and "Space Aliens Learning English," *Poetry Society of Virginia*
"One Day in the Summer," *Bottom Shelf Whiskey*

To Chris and the boys, gratitude for your patience and inspiration. For Paul Witcover, Katy Munger, Randy Fertel, Doris McGehee, Sarah Knorr and her sisters Anne and Ginger, T.J. Cardella, Rosemary Rawlins, the Pietsch's, and everyone else who has encouraged me to put pen to paper, bless you.

I'd also like to express thanks for the poetry reading series at St. Stephen's Episcopal Church here in Richmond, VA, for regularly bringing in such remarkable poets from all over.

SNAPSHOTS

A FISH STORY

I like a life
that grasps life,
one tipped a bit
to the instinctive
side,
that will dare the
touch of an
          other.

I like Daddy cornering
a carp
      pausing
           still as a stump
          arm-diving
            scooping the
               yard of
                  fish
                    from the pool
        a raving
         urgent
     muscle
and tossing again to cool freedom in the slipping
    water.

I like the background
the one that threw him
in four feet of water
four feet long
      heels up

          on a fish's back

and all the brothers
laughing –

like I say
the balance
slightly
          tipped.

NOCTURNE –
AUDUBON PARK

A mist seemed
to raise
the park ethereally

upon some
realm of spirit
unpiqued

in the lucid
light
of day.

A thin swath
half as high as
some of the trees

which spread
out of
the vapor

like scattered
crumbling
monuments

of a forgotten
race, lost
upon this

translucent
plain –
a gift

of the sky
spread sensuously
beckoning

along the dreamed
terrain of
a golf course

at moonset.
That evanescent
radiance

clarified my
level of the
evening

condensing
ground fog
to a phrase

of autumn
sung after
midnight.

Black to infinity
the sky
a promise

to me, as to them,
of the serene
beauty

of emptiness.
And the moon
a comforting

guide
retreated to
a western corner

preparing to leave
me to my senses
reassuring

me, as them,
of the fullness
of aloneness.

There is here no
inkling
of the street

its stolid
shadow and form
its concrete

usual distinctions.
Only this sonorous
call to forget

awaft in a
pageant lit by
moonbeam

this generous
majesty of
soaring

seamless
essential –
There is no word.

I found
myself
later

at the damp
edge of
a yawning

sandtrap,
naked and
steaming

still, though
the moon had
departed

at the end
of my little
dance

in the midst
of a fog,
like theirs,

lost
unschooled
and forgotten,

but calling from
certain
unconscious

kingdoms to
awaken in
the mists

and dance
the moon to
its rest

to risk
once a familiarity
with the source
of the poem.

DEVOTIONAL

Seep in staid winter
gray the whites of my table
ease in sad sky shade the leaves to brown
flit through cold birds leave the seeds to the hardy
rest grass
fade now on the prickly ground.

Wear boots old woman
on the way to the laundry
curl tight young pup sleeping under the house
blow loud slow ship outwit the foggy river
burn hot
green logs not out.

What makes us think
there will be an end of winter?
What light suggests an easing of the rain?
Just that we hear it has always occurred
we hold
more faith than we claim.

LIBERTY UNDER REPAIR

Her cage recedes
half-stripped she looks
to Brooklyn
arms raised above the
tinkerers catch
her torch a glint
of morning sun.

An
old man toeless
pissed his pants
asprawl a
prime bench --
agog the lunchtime
crowd allows his
smell its space.

You can't
forgive the financiers
but at sunset from
their windows whitecaps
lapping Battery
Park itself
seems the low
prow of some
ferry pushing out to sea.

We are
here at nightfall still
weighing these
towers her torch
then chastened
grin : a teenager
sits her boyfriend
in the Battery's
caverned window
                    ass agleam.

WHEN

A dime-
sized
sand crab
skirts
its lair

seagulls
kite the range

pauses there
in mortal
peril

courage?
fear?

When your
time comes

you will be
so strange.

WEEKEND DADDY

in a one-room
flat with a
sofa and lamp
tv and cat

on the wall like
those sacred
pictures of Jesus
in Catholic homes
hangs one photograph
of a 3-year old
with little teeth

FASHIONS OF THE TIMES

A ragged man mournfully
studied the face
of a girl in a magazine.

He knew her or had
known someone so fair?

Grimy fingers at her cheek
slick with the printed sheen
brushed away the ugly words
on her head, he said,
I stack paper
on this grate to
watch it swirl.

PAPER CUP

Hey man gimme a nickel!
Hey girl gimme a
squeeze!

Bench bent
sun tarred
hole in the bottom
Adam

Hey dog gimme a bone!

ON THE L

If that ain't the way

it is: a one-legged man

reading *Steps to Christ*

PAYDAY WITH MY DAD

Raining the beers he had to now
so he opened the passenger door
swung out one leg
and took a long piss
at the drive-in teller's window
before the line of waiting cars.

FOR BORGES

(See the second version of this poem on page 117.)

WALKING IN SNOW
(after Stevens)

Just as white is the absence
of color & the time it takes
to sift into view then
settle lost in
a drift is a breath,
the slog to don
boots and a scarf
earmuffs and wistful
make tracks for an hour
on water made crystal
then epaulets
on burdened limbs
is to shudder (a little)
at all that is hidden
and all that will soon be gone.

FLURRIES

Flurries
pixillate the nabe   Why call them flakes
3-D the space   these dots and jots
between us.   some feather fat
                            that yet dodge your tongue?

They land and shatter
or skitter and roll
maybe hover an instant
perch on a weed.   They bare the invisible
                                    whim of a breeze
                            a fleet sprite spun
                    white gauze in the trees.

Though weary our eyes apprise anew
though chilled enlivened we dare the quip
to light on a realm we know not of
and what if this time it sticks?

FOR LORINE

Snow lit
bare breasts
blue suffused

the breakfast cups

HIGH COOS

In the Woods

Attend as you stroll
a forest path after rain:
Snare played with brushes.

In California
we camped among the redwoods:
Cathedral whispers.

In the Stacks

Basho said to Issa,
"Make a poem be a painting."
Issa winked, "You bet."

Why so many frogs
in old Japanese haiku?
They go plop, so what?

In the News

The look on her face
when the President walked by:
Unripe persimmon.

It was a nice day
even got to work on time
but then the shooter.

In the Window

The problem with time
people always imagine
they've got more than they….

If hate is just fear
spewed out onto some others
then what about love?

In the Air

Do butterflies forget
their almost Rockette
caterpillared strut?

YOU KNOW ME

To find this swan
of origami
in the subway.

Knew I'd see

the fingered twist and squeeze
of a broker Japanese

whose days are shaped by paper
smile at his little caper:

Out of garbage a swan
in the subway set free!

He dropped a poem
you picked it up
and brought it home to me.

DOOR TO THE FLOOR

When I shut off the light another appeared
like a louvered door to the floor
running south to north at the foot of our bed.

In that tremulous hour when I woke and tossed
got up with my twanging frets, what's that?
The door was gone, another imprinted
exactly the same but beamed down now
from the west-facing pane, a tic then a toc
of that slow lunar trek.

Which helped somehow re higher tossings
than my own, that roil in the night
in that place we call space.
It's good to feel small.
It helps to be barred by a rectangle
of moonlight in your windows.
That finger pointing here then here
that marks your place, conducts
along these lines a silent lullabye:

Now sleep and heal, awaken and reel.
If tomorrow the sky is clear
I'll peek in again to tuck you in
tut-tut your swollen fears.

THE EMPTYING

A practiced twist of her thumb
taught you handmade gavadeel.
Now she turns a spoon in her hands
wondering what it might be for.

On a slushy street with a gimlet eye
she purchased baccala and eel
for her Feast of Seven Fishes
we tried to emulate this year.

Love is a gift you share
in the work and the teaching you do.
But when the "how to" has sifted
out of your head what is left
to be done or said?

Angelina born in Italy
a century ago,
think of all she's forgotten
all that she's seen….

Dear grandma, great grandma:
When rosary-entwined
your hands lie still
may your last words be
Marone a mi.

ALZHEIMER'S POEM

(   )

IS THERE LIFE ON MARS?

Today we posit
building blocks.
Rudiments. Let's say
H_2, CO, NH_3.

Now recommend
a toppling
of their compounds,
reversion to
potential.

And ponder
what else
is needed there
that we neglect
in our reductions

to stack this
tower so high
that it wobbles.

YARNS

YOUR PEACH AND MINE

Maybe you rose
from scented sheets
fingered by louvered shades
to a saucer with mint sprigs
and the turgid flesh neatly
sliced of a single perfect peach
each day of an air-conditioned
summer. *Was that our purpose?*

Boots laced against the snakes
shirts cinched to the collar
against the itch in old lady hats
that haloed our necks in shade
we reached with netted poles
teetered on leaning ladders
and tugged against the surly spring
of a motherly branch, cupping
them in our palms tenderly
releasing them to baskets
as if they were eggs. Until the
sun turned peach in setting.

You could say that. But my
guess is that you have forgotten
those tedious mornings, having
to swim or call a friend to make
a day. While we meet in the shade
of a long-shuttered shed unfold
our knives and as the juice

streams down our wrists laugh
at how sick we'd get by end of day
having fed and watered ourselves
on the wind-fallen bee-sucked
weed-nested bruised too
ripe to share with you.

If we are what we do : if our days
add up to anything, then you
can have the wisp a chlorined pool
recalls. Give me that buzzing
morning, a thousand times repeated
that feeds a reeling harvest each time
I sniff a peach.

IMMIGRANT REFLECTION

In my country
we only dressed for church
and let our privates dangle
otherwise. We studied
the webs of spiders, the
flight of swallows, the
whims of the wind.

We never learned much.
How to catch a fish.
How to dip in dance.
How to wait out the weather.

Back there we thought
that was enough. We
honored dogs, fed them first,
sprawled in the sun and tried
to howl in greeting.

We had some rules. People
brought things they'd found
to church and took other
things home. Sometimes
just a smooth rock or a flower
or a feather.

It was like touch chess here.
If you picked it up you had to
keep it and if you brought

it back the next week
people shook their heads.

But nobody would bite you,
not for that. I left before
I learned how we reproduced.
Maybe the same as here, dipping
and howling. I'm trying to
figure it out. What's
different, what's the same.

I'd go back. It doesn't seem
right to wear jeans all day
scrunched on a sofa out of the sun.
I miss my dog. But I'll
get over it. It's part of the game.
I gave this girl a pebble
and she smiled.

IF IT SERVES

Feeling contrary
that night at the observatory
we looked down instead
found a latch to a room
where the projector and its timer
played the ghosts that stalk our woods
the speaker that whoops
its echo in the trees
that busloads come to see and hear
with gifts and totems and tufts of hair
the musty place so long abandoned
its makers lost in the mist.

I said, "It's all a lie!
What a total scam!
We have to let them know!"

But you shot me that look --
yes, that look was a gift that said,
"No, why would you? Leave it so."
Wiped away grime at the skylight
to see them twirl and marvel
their lanterns like bobbing fireflies.

But no, I must have dreamed that.
Went back later and could not find the door.
In the dark, though, an image played on my face,
pilgrims said I seemed inspirited, they touched me.

So then I grasped your reticence.
You don't remember, do you?
But, of course it was a dream!

When you said, with a shrug,
as you turned down the path,
"In the end, what does it matter
if this pageant in the woods
is just some artist's cartoon?
If the only gods we know
are simply handmade projections?

I mean, after all, if it serves?"

FIGMENTS

The wooden boat shook
when the tethered whale
wrenched to slap its tail.

I held onto that memory
for as long as it took
to navigate the stairs
one creaking knee now the other.

And then of course the racing car
with the seatbelt stuck or was it
the fire in my hair or the beach
made of ice cream?

They all seemed so real
at the time. Like you,
the way you tossed your hair,
that guttural thing that thrilled,
the figgy flavor of your meaty lips,
even the sling of your shoulders
stepping sharp up the street.

If we crossed paths again
would we recognize each other?
Would it all come surging back?
Because now trying to remember
I'm making it up just like at dinner
when the family dips its heads and sighs

and I fret over the whale the car the flame the beach
if that is what they were when they occupied
the whole world between my ears.

HOW TO CARRY SOMEONE WHO IS
UNCONSCIOUS

Why would you want to do that?
Is he lying in the street or halfway in a door?
Do you hear gunshots? Do you see blood?
Can you detect a breath
tickle the fine hairs of your ear?
Did you see him fall? Are the two of you alone?

Don't take forever with it – think!
It's okay to drag him, if he's big and you can.

But here's how:

Roll her over on her back
then reach in at her head and push her up
to sitting. Take your time with this, don't hurt yourself,
don't pull her arms, don't tug, remember your back.
Maybe you end up on your knees
so your whole front is like a seat back
for this insensate person. I mean,
you have to understand, this is an intimate maneuver.

But you're only just beginning, so.

Slide your arms under theirs and clasp your wrists at their
    chest.
Make your arms a belt around them, like a big old bear
    hug.

Then if you can do this, here's a place where you need to
    be sure,
get up on one knee, then you and this person
you are hugging tighter than you can believe
use your legs not your back your bodies really sandwiched
you both yes that's right come to a stand.

This is no joke.

Because now you're committed.
Now you could both go down.
It's like a dance, a kind of shuffle
where you squeeze him even tighter
while you shift your position
sidle around to his side somehow -
you really have to practice -
and his sleeping arm you have to duck under
so its hanging out there zombie-like across your shoulder
but what you're going for is to block his knees with yours
shove them up straight and locked
so for the first time you see how tall he is
in this high and tottering precarious place
where you've arranged yourselves.

But that's not even all. Are you ready? Get ready.
Because now comes the switch. No, seriously,
this is how you do it.

It's the weak link in the procedure.
You have to quit the bear hug
while you ease around to her front
and grab her floppy wrists

(it helps to lean forward and crouch
so she sort of drapes across your back)
and then here we go, alright, this is it.

Get in right under their armpits
pull their arms over your shoulders like a shawl,
bend those knees, stick out your butt
(their head may loll or knock onto yours)

and take a tentative step. You've got him.
You can shuffle off to what you hope is safety,
to help, to some kind of better place.
Maybe his legs are long and drag behind,
toes drawing lines from there to here
if you're in sand. People may see you
and not know what to think.

But let me say this. There is a rule
that we all follow and will hold you to.
Oh yes we will. If she is unconscious and you touch her.
If you dare to move her sleeping form.
Until you get her the help she needs and can
do this whole thing we just rehearsed
    entirely in reverse,
until that moment when you step back,
unkink your knees and spine,
wipe at your shirt and bend gasping at her side
until then -- because you touched her --
you own what happens. You are the responsible
party. The Good Samaritan.
In ways you must decide to bear
that is your burden too.

So this. It helps to be ready, to have a clue.
It's not for everybody. I get that.
There are these risks involved
if you dare to cross that line, if
you stop and bend to touch.
You would hope if it was you. But
I'm not here to judge. Which is
why we practice. So here.
A little rude but I call it
try before you buy.

SPACE ALIENS LEARNING ENGLISH TURN TO THE PAGE THAT STARTS WITH *COLONEL BLIMPISM* AND ENDS WITH *COLORWAY*

Discovering that
a phenomenon
of light or perception
is how we distinguish
otherwise identical
things, and that this
inflection named
color is often used
among humans
in that way.

Though some are
color-blind, it seems
and others call others
colored, and those
without *color* – because
the definition of color
*excludes the phenomenon
of light we call white* --
these whites block
those with color
(But why? And how?)
*from participating
in various activities.*

Color bar/color line.

Why would the

colorless -- ie,
pallid, blanched,
dull, uninteresting –
do such a thing?

And how do they
distinguish anyway?
Is that what this thing
a *colorimeter* is for?
Are there *colorists*
who decide? Do they
fear those with something
called *color temperature?*
Blackbodies that can emit
radiant energy to evoke color?

That's it! (They say.)
We've got it. The key's
right here on this page.
Now we know what moves
them. And the word we'll
use when we go down
to *colonize.*

SUBVERSIVE SCRIBBLE: 2069

I've tried to imagine trees.
Thin giants with boisterous heads
mirrored in down-reaching tendrils
and filmy almost translucent
solar panels unfurled along their limbs.

A protective layer called bark
sometimes scaly or it could be smooth as skin.
And their only movement was in growth
each year of the sun adding a ring of width,
some meters to their up yearn to the sky
and down stretch in the nourishing soil.*

They lived as long as (some longer than) we do.
Cradled all sorts of mythical beasts – beetles,
bees, a quick thing called a squirrel, even those
with feathery wings and pointy toes.**

But let's focus just now on the one
tree and then another near it.
Some say they spoke among themselves
feeding oxygen to the sky their aspiration
a gift of breath to us oh here we go again.

Why do all my musings come back
to this our crime? To learn truly too late
what we might have known all along
that recollection cannot match the
thing remembered. That death

comes slowly until it doesn't. That
more goes with the rustling of leaves
than their undeciphered whisper.
I can almost imagine a tree.

  *Next week's imaginative reflection.
**See annual celebration of Earthian Nature.

ONE DAY IN THE SUMMER

Huckleberry Hound was a lazy pup
but rounded the corner with raving eyes
lathered and frantic, like he was pursued.

Said, "Mama, he went up under the house."

"Go get him," she said. "Yes, ma'am," I replied.

Dog-sized chink in the brick foundation
but if I reached one arm in tucked my head
could squirm up follow him into the dark.

She handed me a flashlight, said, "Go on."

This was something I'd never considered
the guts of the house its underbelly

squared onto a powdery dirt that for
all the age of the structure had not seen
the light of day. Dank dry dust and cobwebs
creepy and cool is why he'd gone in there.

It took a while but that had to be Huck
against the blank concrete wall of the porch.
Paired red dots way back there his trembling eyes
or was that just what my eyes were doing?

"Go on now," she said. "Dang, mama, alright.
On my belly toes dug in had to keep
from bumping my head on the kitchen pipes
then past them like diving under water.

Heard him whimper or again it was me
but closer now squeezing midway under
the dining room far up in there was a
private place like nowhere I'd ever been.

Hi ol' Huck.

Eye to eye it was bad how he panted
neck strained teeth bared in a grin that scared me.
Far back in the day Mama said, "Get him."
But this was my call. I said, "Hush Mama."
She didn't like that. "Don't you hush me boy."

Who knows how long it took? Flicked off the light
dropped my head on my arms. I knew one tune
and sang it. Maybe you know the song, too?

Jesus loves the little children
All the children of the world
Red and yellow black and white
They are precious in his sight
Jesus loves the little children
Of the world.

I did that a while like a lullaby.
Then this moan shut me up a whole 'nother
song that right now scribbling can hear it plain.

A lot of time in there to contemplate
the dirt to consider the ticking dark
nose pressed in things I hadn't thought about.

When I dared to switch on the light again
Huck was different, ribs still, legs stretched out
like he was running someplace, eyes bugged, tongue
lolled long and dry. So then what's the hurry?
In that weird space I sang to him some more.

A slow drag then feet first for both of us
snot slimed to mud on my cheeks shirt rode up
and the rub of the dirt at my belly
press of the house like the flat of a hand
freaked out beneath the dangling kitchen pipes
desperate old drowning man flailing for air
little kid squirming to drag a dead dog.

At the hole, worked my legs out first but then
got stuck halfway and yelled. Mama had gone
back inside. She had work to do no time
for my triflin'. That was a lesson too.
Sharp brick drew a long red scratch up my back
but wiggled out one fist tight on a paw
to finally drag him into the light.

Huck was heavy and stiff like all dead things
and dirt had kicked up in his startled eyes.
I said "I'm sorry" and tried to wipe them
my thumb on an eyeball hard as a marble.
Oh man how I hated that scary hole.

Mama came out laid a rag on his back
and spread it to almost cover his legs.
Said, "Huckleberry was a good old pup."
Said, "Prob'ly old man Rufus and all his
durn chickens," whatever she meant by that.

When Daddy got home my dog disappeared.
He mortared up the crawl space too but missed
the new one as fathers do opened up
in me where Huck and I to this day lie
flat in the dark far in and away right
up against the hard fact and singing
as best we can.

BLACKBERRY MISSIVE

July afternoon in Virginia
our father skips lunch
to stride the dry pasture
in work brogues
to that thicket
where blackberries
sprout like purple
polkadots and
wades into the briars
and bees until
sweated out
with knuckles
and forearms bleeding
he's filled two gallon
buckets. Why?

Because we love cobbler.

One of the things
the war took out of Daddy
you'd have to guess
was trust in saying much.
So what if he never
told me that thing,
I mean what's the worth
in words when you
can taste it like that?

SMALL STEPS, '69

Daddy said yes to the pool with that girl
so I finished the sign *Watermelons*
for Sale: $1.00: that green and red slice
made a half-moon with bug-like LEM on top

Oh my in that frilly bikini then
her slim legs churning the bubblegum sheen
of that ramshackle motel's lukewarm pool
on I guess my first sorta halfway date?

Hair damp and heart thumping back at the store
we locked the door for an hour not to watch
but to buy eggs sold cheap down a dirt road
in the woods. Was the truck's radio on?
Pretty sure I knew it was coming up,

but Daddy didn't seem to care a whit.
It would happen or not was just his way.
Something else the war had schooled him over
that he couldn't unlearn is what I think.

The eggs rattled between us on the seat
while I sniffed the chlorine on my fingers
and in my hair and the dust plumed behind
I'd like to imagine all the way up

to where those clunky boots we later learned

stepped down from a ladder to a sea where
even now on full moon nights it all seems
jumbled up like something I must have dreamed

thin legs that splatter a pool's blue water
fat cleats imprinting a virgin beach
in the eggshell gleam of the moon's reflection
half forgotten, except everything's changed.

MAP

Fingers glide
along the
tightening strand
of one long hair
found on my desk

curves, somehow
like the undulations
of a road that travelled
belie a line on a map

one strand, its
tendency at curl,
commits a landscape
to my touch

unfolding
the swells and swales
the hills and breathless
rifts
a tour
of your flesh.

This morning began
like driving fast
sea on the wind
a fog, soft shoulders
the slope and shift
of a winding road

so you gasp and
laugh and shiver.

We were Highway One
to each other
all the way up the coast
'til the seals barked.

Over whiskey
at midnight
awaiting your return
one strand tugged
between my fingers
its tendency at curl
is all the map
an avid traveller
desires.

THE THING ABOUT DOGS

Ginny squats at the tree line
beside not on the trail
then bounds ahead
tail high and wagging:
Who knows what our walk
may bring? A squirrel, a deer,
once tortoises mating, his
chest plate flat and scraping
her helmeted back,
reptilian paws squirming
for purchase and she
seeming to smile patiently
allowing the one thrusting
intrusion her armor
would ever allow. We
animals — how alien
to each other yet how much
in our yearning alike!

Or that other time
Ginny came bolting back
tail between her legs
because behind her loped
at twenty paces
in no special hurry
a coyote bony
as the wily cartoon
in chilling pursuit

her cousin – what all dogs
would be, I guess,
without us.

Most days it's just
a trudge I hardly register.
She romps ahead then
waits on her haunches
my guide and example
wondering why he can't seem
to forget himself for one minute.
I mean, how much better to
nose about, to sniff the riches,
all the variants from yesterday's
adventure, oh here, see this
dead branch has fallen!

Begrudge an hour after work.
Let the girl off leash to run,
let me off keyboard to stroll,
and stretch our legs.
Big deal.

Exactly. Because
in the best of all possible
futures – we have just
4 or 5 short human years
before this will be too much
for her. Her fluffy coat
thinned, her muzzle grizzled
and yes how I will cry

that day we lay
her ashes here.

Because then you know
all these mundane walks
that mean nothing
but catching the air
will rise past goals and
objectives and balanced
books to strike me
hard across the face.

While all I fret over, my
schemes and worry my
grudges and drudgery
add up to less
than that cobweb
brushing my cheek back
when Ginny's tongue lolled
so giddily on her frolic
ahead on a woodsy
lane and oh too late
I hear it now the world
at my knee said, woof.

DON'T LET THIS HAPPEN TO YOU

I had not seen him in the decade
since our father died
during which my sons grew to teens
and his gave birth to a granddaughter.

The house to which I'd condemned him
stood rickety, junk burdened, the kitchen
floor caved in and half-repaired, the whole
place small, smelly, abandoned feeling.

And he – I hadn't knocked – on a sofa
pulled up to the fire and a flat panel,
the back of his head that hay-like blond
streaked now with grizzled gray atop
a thick and flannelled road-mapped neck.

I said, "Greg" and he stood up sheepish
from the Solitaire game on his laptop
almost as if he'd expected me, and why not?
So we played it that way, and I gave him
the hard cider I'd brought, asked how
the Steelers were doing on the screen, led him
back out to the mini van where the lean and
scraggly teens he'd last seen as roly-poly
toddlers sat wondering if they'd ever
been here.

How I hope they never will.

Because it is a shameful thing
when brothers turn away from a childhood
spent in superhero capes, running post patterns,
climbing trees, building forts from wood piles,
playing itchy games of hide-and-seek in acres of tall corn.
When they pick a fight and call it done.
Find it easy to go on not even a card at Christmas time.

For some reason, I asked about our old tree,
had dreamed that week that it fell
on our childhood home, crushing the red-tiled roof
like the hand of God disgusted. He said, it's still there
and so it was, but in its dotage, the low branches where
we'd plotted our cowboy schemes rotted off, the
limb where our rope swing had swung. The grand old
    maple
was beginning to split down the middle, half tipping
towards the house, half tipping away, and someone
at some point, would have to make a decision
to take it down or see my dream lived out.

I said, call me will ya. He said he would.
You should see my granddaughter. She's a pistol.
I said I bet she is. He stood there in flannel bottoms,
barefoot in the wet grass, my little brother, taller
by a head than me. I saw him, though, at 5 and
frail, with hair like dandelion gone to seed,
the boy I'd loved, protected, taught, half-raised.
Who would never, I knew, pick up the phone.

So got in the car and turned it around. He was
already gone inside. To stoke the fire. To open

that bottle and swig the flavor of apples with a kick, shake
   his head, awaken his laptop and settle
into the game. At dusk his wife and high school
   sweetheart Sandy will come home
from her shift at the restaurant, and he'll say,
I saved you some. Where'd you get that?
Weird. Old Tony came by. Huh, she'll answer,
hand at his shoulder.
Brought you some chicken. What'd he want?
Who knows, left this bottle. I'll be.
Oh hey, the Steelers win?

RAVES

PLACES I STILL AM, NO. 4

There is a trick to blowing bubbles
but like so many things you'll learn
in life, where everything is bubble
fragile, it's easy once you get it.

That measured puff –
Its reward your own hot breath
packaged in a glistening globe
and floating oh so buoyantly
with its fellows on a current
you can't otherwise see
before of a sudden expiring
with a silent pop at the prick
of a blade of grass.

Somewhere in my childish heart
I glimpse a glint of the lesson there:

Blow more and more until
the breeze across our yard
is flagged with bobbing spheres
that stir a sort of expectant glee
there not there, exactly!
And the little bottle it came in
gone finally empty, too.

RIVER SHADOWS

Have you seen
the somber
loom of winter
trees lay stripes
on clear water --
maybe a trout
stream
after snow?

The penciled
line jagged
along the
rocky bed
overdrawn
by a skittering
rippled lid

like time
what flows
like hurt
what won't

a day underway
a smudge beneath
that will not
budge or sway

the current ignites
and scatters
the shadows
lay down the law

or is it two truths
that interplay
you go you stay
stubborn rule
that cannot hold
the flow at bay?

BIRDS IN SNOW

Birds in snow don't flit they dart
missiles fueled by feathered hearts
aimed at shelter suet or seed
never falter in their need
to go and get and seek and weather.
You do it too in fleece and leather.

Though we pretend to art and awe
logic wonder prayer and law
we emulate our feathered friends
in how we mark the time we spend.
When wintry wind
and snow descend
what it takes to get 'er done
is all that matters to anyone.

THE POET'S WAY

Whenever I wake up in the middle of my life
and notice something
and notice it enough to write it down

old man Allen Ginsberg told the tv screen

gifts are rare and come of themselves
your main task is to record your consciousness.

THE LEFT BEHINDS

"Horses fuck inside me."
Think how the women who read that
must have lined up outside Frank Stanford's door.
But then you scrawl such a thing
I mean if you mean it
well you know how it ends.

Anybody who followed Anthony Bourdain
as far back as *Kitchen Confidential*
had to see where he was headed
yet like Stanford the thing is:
Such vigor! Such heart!
So opposite all that!

Or take the radio ear worm
I don't have a gun
I don't have a gun
I don't have a gun
Did no one think to check?

That other song *People Who Died*?
I've lost just as many, you maybe too.
Not war, my generation threaded that needle
somehow, it was other stuff
like what Jim sang, and then
he added that killer PS.

Was that song his hint?
I mean the only thing we know

is what Keanu Reeves replied
when asked what happens after death:
"The people who love you will miss you."

Yes. But this if you're contemplating --
and let me first say please reconsider:

They'll also bear the yoke of their failure
to decode your signal instead of grooving on
all that diversionary static, your hypnotizing
saraband that only in retrospect seemed
to protest too much.

THE DEPRESSIVE
ENUMERATES

My chest
is a screen door
through which the wind
spaghettis

Dangles from my back
like worms
when I walk.

My head
is a transom
through which the light
confettis,

drifts to my feet
like photos
of snow.

My hands
are spiders
my dick
a tv
my knees
are clocks
my shoulders
a shelf

my mind an old hog
that roots through
the middle
snuffling and snorting
digesting itself.

IT'S JUST HOW I AM, RIGHT?

What if love, like light
is an oceanic emanation
and my heart, like my eyes
can glimpse only some of the waves?

What instrument or theory
or tilt of the head might help me
apprehend a wider band
of the spectrum?

I'm not saying comprehend,
I'm not that vain
but just to bathe in it
to adore the way hawks see.

What if it's here and it's just
how I am:
clouded by cataracts
feeling by touch
toeing along
on the sand?

IT'S EASY TO FRET OVER FAILURE

It's easy to fret over failure. It's American as apple pie.
I do it. Every time an old classmate makes the *Times*.
Roads not taken, opportunities waved away, fear.
You look back and can't imagine what brought you here.
A faded Kodak with the rippled edges of a fat boy
smug in a row of cousins in a jumble of plastic toys
looking into the lens and the face behind it with just -
Well you can read what you want in that pudge,
a hint of the tremble to come in the chin, the creases
at the eyes. They call that callow youth, who sees
the highway not the ruts, the pie and not
the rolling pin, the venison not the guts.
Except, that something in the chin and lips,
a shadow at the eyes, checking the box for a slip.
I guess that was me, but who can say?
And the thing is, what you forget today
is where you were, what mattered when the call came.
You forget that you knew epiphany by name,
threw off your clothes on mountaintops and sang.
Sought what seemed true at the time, what really rang
beyond the phone. Maybe you ran on heart,
misjudged, screwed up, never knew where to start.
Maybe you didn't do your best, never found your voice.
Threw days away and friends like so many plastic toys.
Figured that ending up tired at dusk meant a job well done.
Figured that leaving any place only meant you'd gone.
It's easy to fret over failure. To think of what might have
    been.

It's easy to stitch up a different life with different
    decisions
that add up to wins. If you'd turned to the mountains
    instead of the coast.
If you'd partied less and studied most.
If you'd followed the road that ran through the trees
instead of the one that seemed, for you, a breeze.
It's easy to fret and easy to wince at
what's left of you today, when at last you glimpse
through the camera lens a telescoped perspective
to the choices you'd make, the chances you'd take,
in a fat boy on the floor among relatives.

THE DAZZLEMENT

Boy no more than six stares right through me dead center
front row among all the other kids at Vacation Bible
School in a knit shirt that doesn't quite meet his pants
brilliant eyes eager smile he could tell you the answer
right now and you would listen and know he was
absolutely correct and would join in his march the whole
world waiting for his nod and all a playground he the
cardboard-sword wielding captain of these buzz cut
squirrelly sugar snaps stuffed and restless youngsters
seedlings any minute now to be tossed up and scattered
helter-skelter upon the earth to thrive and propagate and
swish like wheat in the wind but he among the mass of
them the one you would watch would bet on because you
know not height nor heft nor even wealth can overtop that
sparkling intelligence that curiosity that expectant joy he
clearly radiates not just this June morning in 1960 but
certainly every day of his short unspooling life you just
want to walk over and give him a good burning noogie rub
off some of the luck on yourself and you think he would
even understand and not hold it against you though hating
how you held and wrestled him there in your overweening
unfair strength and stature tinged with a smudge of
jealousy for this little kid who knows something you
forgot or maybe never even dreamed when you were his
size and certainly not now after so much water under the
bridge but really you just want to dive into the scene go
black and white if you have to two-dimensional kneel
before all the lined up kids and one by one give each a hug
and maybe a shiny quarter tell them what they possess

what pulses breathes leaps and burgeons within them a
song called potential a song called yes and now all of them
of course but this one kid you've been eyeing who's been
eyeing you back without any hint of a flinch he's the one
who breaks you the one you can't you're so afraid that if
you reach out if you rest a hand on his narrow shoulder it
will all evaporate the first real magic you've ever paused
to appreciate or write this sprawling hymn to you want to
apologize for so much for how you failed him for turns of
events for cowardices for misgivings and mistakes he
would never have made yet did when the time came when
the earth he naturally ruled grew rough like gravel to his
sneakered feet when the air smelled of burning rubber and
the church bell rope snapped high up in the steeple but
people just shrugged and let the old bell rust and he did
too oh boy in this picture I adore you yet clueless what to
do so much too late now to repay this debt you're owed
for seeing how lollipop sweet it all could be for knowing
the dazzlement that it is for standing there grinning
straight back at the camera ready to take it all on.

TRUISMS

We thought, I guess, that we could pretend it was all just a
tv reality show on a station we didn't get. Where they
jack boys (and girls) up on *5-Hour Energy* shots, wrap
them in *Kevlar* and canvas, and drop them in the desert
with weapons out of space movies to rampage or
whatever. Where some nerd in a silo in Charlottesville
steers a joystick swabbed with steri-wipes, what the
President calls surgical strikes, which just means
somebody else does the cleanup. The frakking channel,
the oil shale channel, the hole in the ocean floor channel.
The mystery series: bee deaths, whale beachings,
backyard coyotes, polar bear strandings, fire ants, the
waning of butterflies. To us it's senseless: the campus
gang rapes, the trigger-happy cops, the arsonists, students
with automatic rifles gone rogue, the suicides, the cancers
buying radiologists condos. We buy better locks, rig
cameras in the garage, work two jobs when we can find
them. We do get that the circle of those we can trust
dwindles by the year. Old farmer's sayings we've
forgotten or snort at, beer bubbling from our snouts.
Platitudes. Truisms. Things like, chickens come home to
roost, reap what you sow, red sky at morning, the whole is
greater….

PROVISIONS

But what could it mean, seriously, y'know, well, when you think, it's just, you start in, and I think, in the whole scheme of things, uh, it's, the whole scope, the range, I mean, now, it seems like, to our knowledge, what I heard, anyway, but actually, it should only be in the case of, it's just a way, it's important to, it comes up, it arises, unprompted, they're saying, the main thing, historically speaking, when you consider, interestingly, from a global perspective, across the board, I have this concern that, under certain circumstances, without a doubt, one would assume, when you really think about it, indubitably, we might be able to, over and above, just one thing, at the moment, to be sure, I feel like, moving on, if anything, what we have here, my thought would be, for instance, would you say, for example, for me, the point is, are you implying, in the world today, at this point in time, so, it could be that, like, hold on a minute, wait, I thought the idea was, just so you know, looking ahead, looking back, look, as opposed to, supposedly, sometimes, from time to time, the way things are, thus far anyway, oh man, OMG, most of the time, I was wondering, of course, the situation is, let me ask you this, in general, specifically, you might say, mark my words, listen, if we just, I don't know but, see?

THE DAWN OF SOMETHING
(Added line breaks to an Amazon review of a Tao Lin book of poems)

I don't think I
usually like poetry.

I went to a poetry
reading tonight and I
did not enjoy it.

I liked this book.

It was like reading
transcripts of my
own thoughts.
It validated my
thoughts
somewhat I
guess, in letting me
know that other people
thought
similar things, and
that other other
people were publishing
transcripts of them. I

think writing like
this is positive in
that it encourages
calm reflection on one's

own life through direct
analysis of another's.

I feel like an idiot right now.
I have tried to describe why I
like this book.

I like this book.

POEM FOR 2020

I pull off to pee at the Walt Whitman Wayside on the
Jersey Turnpike.
Through the woods from Camden where the poet lived his
last,
where he mused and predicted, dictated and preened,
gazed with dimming eyes out his doorway past the
fragrant lilac vines,
lost in memories of war and men torn and ruined in battle,
wistful dreams of furtive loves, and the epiphany he knew
and had somehow wrought into a book.

He saw what we did to each other. He imagined what we
could be.
He said he would wait for us here.

Along this divided highway, pressed gravel and tar made
macadam smooth
at these exit ramps fingering to Philly and Trenton and
Asbury Park,
home to superhero athletes, devious politicians, poets with
guitars, and all of us who drive.
Stop with me here before the row of drink machines, five
bulky rectangles, side-by-side.
Their clear plastic windows and cans stacked tight: Coca-
Cola, Mountain Dew, Diet Pepsi, Sprite, Dr. Pepper,
Snapple, Red Bull, and 7-Up. All shiny, all sugared, all
bubbly.
All promising some subtle rush, a little rapture, that
impalpable sustenance available to all with a dollar.

Turn to the double doors, swinging open and shut, and the
little glass room they frame.
Funneled through them, in then out, and on down the
turnpike every kind of person.
Pause with me here by the drink machines, loiter and look,
and try to see what he saw.

That little old lady was a teacher, her son is her driver
now, a broker who loves his mom.
That man at the door wears a turban. Is he a Hindu, a Sikh,
a suburban father from Rahway? He looks at his watch.
He nods to us. His father, the immigrant, always so long in
the Men's Room.

Ah, the Men's Room, how this would have stirred the old
bawd! The phalanx of identical porcelain urinals, no
dividers between them, all down the wall. The men side by
side at their business, none looking left or right, so serious,
so private, so mindful to follow that rule.

The rhythmic flushing, almost a beat, the stench of
blended vapors from their voiding, and the jet plane roar
of the drying machines. Eyes askance, fingers at zippers,
feet testing the slippery floor.

And the Women's Room, never enough stalls, the long
line out the door and their mincing needy dance, the fretful
glances and nods of commiseration. I mean, this is the
most democratic place, don't you think?

Are you a casino owner climbing out of your limo in kid
gloves?

Are you a cheerleader off the bus flipping your hair and
stretching?
A trucker en route to Miami?
Do you use a wheelchair?
Do you identify as he or her or them?
Do you make this trip every day, or is this your first
rubber-necking sojourn along the edge of America,
straight off the plane at Newark?
Are you rushing to work, to the game, or are you rushing
because that is what you do?

No, wait, hold up, stand back and groove with me.

Admire the wall of fast food joints staffed with counter
persons and the workers at the back.
Where do they live? Where do they park their cars?
I see you chubby fry cook and the splatter burns on your
arms.
I see you sallow-faced manager, flat-footed, spinning in
place, dreading another breakdown of the ice machine.
You children in your winter coats, like bubbles with faces,
your tiny hands lost in your mothers' mittened palms.

We are Southerners headed home where people drawl, we
are IT specialists who surf on weekends, we are combat
veterans and judges and students with depression
diagnoses. We pour water from bottles for our dogs.

All the coming and going, the thousands streaming, no one
bumping, no one cursing, cats that herd themselves.
And the same in the parking lot, cars backing, waiting,
accelerating out past the gas pumps, past the 18-wheelers

lined up on the side, past the dog walkers and the scraggly
pines and the skittering of trash, one empty can rolling
with a tuneful clatter across the greasy asphalt as rain
begins to fall.
Yo, Wayside named for our Bard with a Capital-B, you
too are the poem he scrawled, and each of us a line.
The hum of our valvèd hearts, the stink of what dumps
from our innards, our greasy lips, the common urgent
fatigue.

The Walt Whitman Service Area as America singing
whether we know it or not.

He wrote: *You may read the President's message and read
nothing about it there. I do not know what it is except that
it is grand, and that it is happiness,* that thing the
Founders urged on us, pursuit pursuit pursuit and an
asphalt grid to do it on. Never the getting there, not for us,
the going is the thing.

He asked, *What is it then between us?* Could this wayside
offer a clue? Well, what if you took me up on this? What
if we paused, stepped out of the way, and peered around
for one minute?

Would we see what the poet promised, would we
comprehend what he meant, would we take that moment
to marvel, and would that be enough?

CORRESPONDENCE

Once I dared
a poem of
several pages

with triplets
in homage to
WCW

that he no
doubt would have
chided.

Though never
published, it
meant so

much to me –
still does.
It nailed

a private
thing I
feel and do

or did
involving
joy.

Today I
came across
a book

of Li Po
poems and
in it found

that same
moon-conjured
dance

penned
by an ancient
Chinese

rascal
the best friend
I never had.

AT THE EQUINOX

Summer ends
with a wail
for some of us.

For most, though,
the calendar fails.

Far along
bundled in sweaters
we cast to a leaf-
muddled fen;
only then land
the fair morning
when our fall began.

CAN YOU HELP ME?

In what one might call my better moments
it seems that the problem concerns
the woeful limitations of my senses,
perceptions, that apprehension like a god's
Shakespeare went on about. It's that thing where
the physicists are on to something
the Buddhists have been teaching all along.

The idea that everything is evanescent, porous, buzzing.
So the closer you look the more it all jiggles, whines,
dissolves, gives up the ghost, you might say.

But then, you ask, why couldn't I slide my hand
into a tree trunk, share its woody yearning
with my own fleshy zest? If it's all aflutter
in that way? And each of us but a temporary solution
to a star dust puzzle apt at any time to go up in smoke?

I kick Dr. Johnson's rock, and that is my assurance
that, hey, it's all about me. What I see and do right now
is where it's at. Which is what we call sanity.
But the truth is that the minute I'm gone this notion
that the world revolves around me will be too.

So my question is: What do I do with that?
Perhaps no god is necessary, but something has to give.
The physicists say calculate, the Buddhists say breathe.
Are those reasonable plans?

Which is why I dedicate whatever is left
of this concatenation I call me
and this waft I call mine to a song and dance
that might count/inspire/expire, that would
in the end maybe reconcile this precious finger snap
we call self with the flash and tumult that goes on.

RULE OF SEVENS

From what I know
of illness and chance
there must be a suffocated
moth in a fisted cocoon

just as there are amputee dogs
living out there allotted
3-legged decade as doggie
as the rest.

And there are grandma's
with breasts made rocky by cancer
who sing at break of day that old
Amazing Grace while a President
flips channels unable to turn off.

The ancient Babylonians
noted five wandering stars
plus the showcase sun and moon
and so we are ruled by sevens
all the weeks of our lives.

Tony Gentry is the author of a novel *The Coal Tower*, short-listed for the 2019 Faulkner Society Prize, and a collection of stories *Last Rites*. He has also authored five young adult biographies (*Paul Laurence Dunbar*, *Jessie Owens*, *Dizzy Gillespie* (winner of 1993 New York Public Library Biography Award), *Alice Walker*, and *Elvis Presley*. Tony holds degrees from Harvard College (BA), New York University (MA), and the University of Virginia (PhD). He is a tenured professor of occupational therapy at Virginia Commonwealth University, specializing in assistive technology for cognition. He lives in Bon Air with his wife Chris, sons Nick and Stephen, and their dog Buddy. Tony blogs at tonygentry.com.

Praise for *The Coal Tower*:

"Piling layer upon layer of life lived on game day Charlottesville-style, Tony Gentry in his debut novel brilliantly weaves multiple plot lines bent toward an uncertain and unexpected catastrophe. Displaying equal parts gusto for language and love of his singular characters, *The Coal Tower* brings to mind two masterpieces of the last century, Virginia Woolf's *Mrs. Dalloway* and Joyce Cary's *The Horse's Mouth*." – Randy Fertel, author of *A Taste for Chaos: The Art of Literary Improvisation*

"*The Coal Tower* has it all: colorful characters, rapid pacing, dark humor, and an unexpectedly moving story. The author has a fond eye for the eccentricities of people, imbuing his debut novel with a basic love for humanity that makes reading it a joy. " – Katy Munger, author of 15 mystery novels

"Like some mutant love child of Cormac McCarthy and John Kennedy Toole, *The Coal Tower* casts a poignant, provocative, and at times hilarious light on the fractured American landscape of today. Tony Gentry's remarkable debut signals the arrival of an incandescent new voice." – Paul Witcover, author of *The Watchman of Eternity*

Last Rites, a story collection:

Ernest Hemingway wrote, "All stories…end in death." With ringing lyricism, cinematic detail, and wry humor, in this diverse collection of tales Tony Gentry interrogates that notion. A father and son share a moment of everyday epiphany on their farm. An elderly widower must choose between a circumscribed life where every breath is an effort and a saving reunion he barely trusts, while another finds solace in the company of an old bear. The ghost of a Confederate general wanders the historic precincts of modern-day Richmond, Virginia. The First Lady deposes the President. A boy finds not love but purpose in a kiss. On a canoe trip, two middle-aged brothers confront mortality and the mystery of what lies beyond. Veterans of the Korean and Viet Nam wars face their demons, seeking reasons to go on. In the longest tale here, a fall from a wheelchair tests the will of a man haunted by the car crash that severed his spine and killed his young daughter years ago. And cancer tells its own origin story, that of a real estate mogul turned megalomaniac. Keenly observed, inventive, and thought-provoking, these stories test the curtain between everyday reality and the tempting whisperings that lie beyond, in that uncanny place where our hearts and minds collide.